The Daily Thoughts of Beans Lee
The Dirty Poet

VOLUME 1:

VIVID SEXUAL POETRY

Beans Lee

CONTENTS

DEDICATION

To myself, for showing up, pushing through, and finishing want I started.

ACKNOWLEDGEMENT

I want to say "Thank You" to my sister Darla Lehnert. For pushing me to get my book done and for answering all my questions along the way. I love you! Blessings upon Blessings!

HEAD WORK

I'm sitting here thinking about your head,

Between my thighs.

You're making my hips rise.

It's making me realize,

How exactly you make me feel inside.

You be taking me on this ride,

You get me so wet,

It's like a slip and slide.

As your tongue opens up my lips,

My kitty cat starts to drip.

As, you start to penetrate,

My legs start to shake.

My nails start to dig into your back,

You have the best tongue game that's a fact.

Now, let's flip the script,

It's my turn to suck your dick.

It's my turn to get in between your thighs,

Making your hips rise.

I gotta make you realize,

My head game is not lame.

I love to get nasty with it,

I don't just suck it, I kiss it, I lick it.

I love to have your balls in my mouth at the same time,

That's why I enjoy deep throating it.

I love when it gets dripping wet.

The best part of sucking it,

Is when you cum,

Cuz, I swallow it all,

Not just some.

I'm going to suck on your balls till you go numb.

Because, I got that yum yum chocolate chip yummy dip,

No boo I don't spit.

FINGER POP

I want to get on top and ride until my legs go numb,

I want you to finger pop my ass hole with your thumb.

Then, I want you to put your dick in my mouth so I can get it dripping wet,

Let's make a bet that I can swallow him whole without gagging one bit,

I can go hours without any compliments.

My mouth is very fit, and no boo I don't spit.

I enjoy this as much as you do.

I love to please, especially when laying between your knees. I love it when you look down at me,

In my eyes and that's when your hips start to rise.

As, you start to moan and grown,

I start bobbing my head faster and faster.

That's when I noticed you tried to climb the wall,

I said boo you're not spider-man you will fall.

I kept going at it until you busted your nut.

Next, you asked if you could fuck me in my butt,

I said of course boo if that's what you want to do.

The look on your face,

I could never replace,

But, I can say I want to do this everyday if that's ok?

KISSED

She leaned over and kissed me and whispered in my ear
"Baby, with you I have nothing to fear."

She said, "I must confess without you I would be a mess"

She said, "I love the things you do to me, can't you see.

You take me on a ride like ecstasy."

She said, "When you eat my pussy you get it dripping wet,
And you have always kept it real since the first day we
met."

I said, "Babygirl, you will forever remain in my world."

You are my sunshine and my rain, without you I feel so
much pain."

But, through it all as long as I have you,

We will be ok boo.

NO FOOL

I must say your dick is just the right size,

It fills me completely in my insides. I can feel him all on my walls,

As I'm slowly rubbing on your balls.

The, look in your eyes makes me realize you love the feeling of my wet pussy,

And, it just keeps getting more and more gushy.

We continue to smoke,

Between each stroke, we get higher and higher.

At this point I wish this moment could last forever.

The love you give me makes me feel like a fen.

And, still to this day you tell everyone that I'm your beauty Queen.

All these thoughts are running through my head,

As you're making love to me in this bed.

You whispered in my ear,

You will never have anything to fear,

As long as you keep me near.

I love every inch of you, and yes all your thick curves too. Then, you grab me around my thighs,

And, in that moment that's when I realized,

We both had cum at the same time.

It was so wet it felt like we were laying in a pool,

I love the fact that you know how to make love and don't need to be schooled,

because I refuse to fall head over heels for a fool.

LIT

The candle is lit, and wax is dripping down the stick.

I'm watching it glow, as I start to lick on you down below.
You look down at me with those dark brown eyes,

You look so amazed and in a daze.

I can tell you love my lips as you start to move your hips
front to back,

So I start deep throating you.

You start to say my name underneath your breath and then
You tell me you love me to death.

I wrapped my arms around your body,

Gripping you so tight,

The glow from the candle gave me just enough light,

To see the biggest smile on your face that night.

I wanted this moment to last forever,

You know I love giving you the best pleasure ever,

Your my boo.

I love you too.

PASSION

A passionate night between me and you

I can't begin to tell you the things I want to do.

First, we can dim the lights and get closer....

I'll kiss your lips that are so sweet, then move on to your cheek, that's so smooth and unique.

Then, I'll move right along that little ear of yours, then let me move down along your chest.

Uh oh, I missed a spot, let me move back up to your neck.

As, I move my tongue around and around you start to feel it as I go down, slowly and as I kiss your chest, your hands go up.....

but I'm not finished yet.

As I move down past your waistline, I begin to kiss, then I woke up realizing this was all a dream, and Damn, was I so pissed

MY LIPS

As I spread your legs apart above my head,

I begin by licking your clit.

I love the feeling of your warmth all over my soft lips.

You, loved how I hummed and you felt the vibrations go up your spine,

Then, I started nibbling, and that's when you started shiver-ing.

That's when you began digging your nails into my back,

Your legs started shaking continuously,

I knew you were about to cum, because the increase of your heart rate.

You took your arms and wrapped them around my neck,

You looked me in my eyes,

And said "Boo, your the only one to please me like that.

I love your head work,

Your one of a kind,

How do I go about making you mine?"

I replied by saying, "Now, it's your turn, to show me what you're about,

And I guarantee that if you can please me the way I did you,

you will forever remain in my world and you will forever be my girl."

DAZED

I'm in a daze, and so amazed of how his fingers roamed my body.

Caressing every inch of my bare skin.

The way his hands perfectly squeezed my breasts as I watched my nipples erect for him.

But, it was his tongue that got me to scream his name, when he licked his way down my body.

Once, he got down to my kitty cat, I knew that shit was a wrap.

He made love to my pussy, got me all wet and gushy.

He started fingering me that's when it felt like I had went pee.

I had squirted all over the sheets, all the way down to my feet.

I left him in a daze and amazed.

US

I'm sitting here thinking about Us laying between the sheets, our heart doesn't ever skip a beat.

Your, arms and legs are wrapped around me like you're giving me a forever hug.

I love the feeling, we're so snug.

I felt your hard dick pressed up against me, oh I knew it was about that time to bump and grind.

You played with the pussy got it dripping wet, and slid him in.

You had your hands wrapped around my waist, I jokingly said, I'm not going anywhere.

You said baby, I know you will never go.

You kept stroking & stroking, getting deeper and deeper, I wanted this moment to last forever, but as soon as you busted a nut, I said next round I want it in my butt.

You said, baby get on all 4's and we can start round 2, baby girl you got me in love with you.

AS I SAT

As I sat upon your Big Thick Dick, my hips started to rise.

And, to my surprise that's when I realized your dick game was good as shit, no wonder why every woman wanted to hit.

I was bouncing up and down, spinning like a merry go round while my pussy was making a wet and gushy sound.

You had one hand on my ass, the other hand lighting up the grass.

As, you continued to smoke between each stroke

Your legs began to shake, I knew you were about to cum,

When you moaned my legs are going numb.

I hopped off your dick real quick,

Put him in my mouth, so I could swallow your cream,

I know my head game is very mean.

Your eyes rolled so far back in your head, I thought for sure you had seen red.

Then, you looked back at me you said " You got the best head game ever, watching you do what you do to me is such a pleasure."

PLEASURE

I'm all about giving my partner the best pleasure ever

Regardless, what they ask for

Behind, a closed door.

Let me name a few, that I will do

I will do 69 for hours at a time and never complain

And, no I'm not insane

They can handcuff me to the bed post

Blind fold me, whip me with leather

Even tickle me with a feather.

They can even slide it in my ass, while grabbing my hair

We can even play a game of truth or dare, and no we don't have to play fair.

Yes, we can have a threesome, as long one is eating my pussy, the other one licking my ass, while I'm smoking my grass.

I have even been asked to fuck a man in the ass

So, that's what I did, I put on my strap on,

I had him moaning my name

Now, that shit is insane.

The next day he was walking with a cane.

But, asking me to do it again.

We can dress up in customs, we can roll play all day

One thing I must say,

You always want to keep your partner happy

So, you must be a lady in the streets

And, a freak in the bed

Always, thinking of new ideas

Continue to go out on dates

So y'all can find some new play mates.

Be your partners everything

There lover and there friend

That way they will be there to the end

DRIPPING WET

I just got out the shower dripping wet

I knew we were about to get it on

I just didn't know what to expect

You opened up your arms

And, I walked over to you

You hugged me so tight, it felt so right

You whispered in my ear, I hope you're ready because it's going to be amazing night.

You, picked me up and layed me gently on the bed

Kissing me so softly, from head to toe

Then, you spread my legs apart

And, started eatin

I knew at that moment I wanted to swallow your semen

And, thats what I did, I started sucking, swallowing him whole, getting deeper in my throat, never wanting to let go.

The sounds of your moans got more and more intense

Then, I took it out and started lickin on your balls

You said, baby, I want to fuck you raw.

19

You got deep in my pussy

Got it all wet and gushy

Had me digging my nails into your back

My man has the best dick game and thats a fact.

I looked you in your eyes

And, to my surprise, you said, Baby, I love you more than you will ever know.

I want this to last forever, I'm never letting go.

I said, " Baby, I'm not going anywhere.

Together, we make one perfect pair.

VISIONS

The visions of you remain in my head, thinking about you laying across your bed.

You staring at me, explaining in details the things you were about to do to me.

You told me to lay back and relax my mind, it was time for me to unwind.

You, were going to light some candles, you were going to pour hot oil and wax on my legs and back.

You were going to rub every inch and every muscle, from my toes all the way up to my neck.

Then, you were going to kiss me from head to toe

Holding me close, and never letting go.

You were going to lick me between my thighs,

Making every inch of my hips rise.

You were going to use your tongue to make love to my pussy,

You were going to get it all wet and gushy.

The more I squirted, the more you wanted some,

You were going to swallow every drip of my cum.

Then, you were going to slide your big thick dick,

In between my phat pussy lips.

You were going to do it doggy style,

With one hand around my neck,

The other holding my waist,

So, you could hold me in the right place.

You were going to moan in my ear,

You were going to moan my name,

You told me sex with you would never be lame.

You were going to bump and grind,

Until you busted your nut,

You were going to take it out,

Then put it in my butt,

You were going to cum all inside my ass,

And, that's exactly what you did,

Word for word,

Inside, your bed.

STRADDLE

As I lay on my back

You straddle on top of me

Fucking my mouth

With your big cock

You wrap your hands around my neck

Grabbing me as you get deeper and deeper

Down my throat

My lips are super soaked.

Your moans got so intense

I knew you were thinking "Damn, this shit makes no since"

You asked if I needed to come up for air

I said No daddy I swear,

It's ok, you don't have to play fair

I breathe through my nose

While your deep throating me

I even continue to suck on you

While replying to you're questions boo

You looked me in my eyes

And to my surprise

You asked if it was okay if you busted your nut

Because, you were ready to flip me over and fuck me in my butt.

I said go head boo, I'm ready for round two

I flipped over

Got on all fours, before I knew it you had me sweating out my pours.

Holding me around my waist line

Pounding my ass

Until, we both busted a nut

You whispered in my ear

A woman like you is so rare

There is no woman I personally know that could compare to you I swear.

ON THE GROUND

As we were rolling around,

On the ground,

We started to make this squishy sound.

The fact that we didn't even care,

That people started to point and stare,

Or, just the fact of them even being there.

Was beyond me.

But, I forgot to mention,

We were naked and all,

And, still having a ball.

We were sucking and fucking,

Licking and sticking,

Moaning and groaning,

The moans got so intense,

You busted your nut right in my butt.

As we are rolling around,

On the ground,

We started to hear that squishy sound.

The fact that we didn't even care,

That people started to point and stare,

Or, just the fact of them even being there.

Was beyond me.

I WANT TO.....

I want to kiss it, lick it, suck it, fuck it

Get it dripping wet

Let's make a bet

I can swallow him whole

Without gagging one bit

No Daddy I don't spit

I love to go for hours

I will even suck it while we are in the shower

Let me get down on my knees

So I can please his wants and needs

I want to kiss it, lick it, suck it, fuck it

Get it dripping wet

Slurping it, jerking it

Rolling my tongue 👅 around it while your eyes roll into the back of your head

I love to hear you moan my name

Telling me my head game is not lame

It's so good it's driving you insane

I want to kiss it, lick it, suck it, fuck it

Get it dripping wet

Let's make a bet

I can swallow him whole

Without gagging one bit

Remember Daddy I don't spit

MY MISSION

This is my mission, to figure out my favorite sexual position.

I like when they're on top,

because they always hit my yum yum spot.

I also like to be held while they're standing,

I be going up and down like a merry go round.

I also like to be the one riding on the top, with my feet up on their chest.

They're looking at me like damn, I must confess, this girl got me fucked up in the head and I'm a mess.

I like it doggy style, while they're pulling on my hair,

as I move my ass cheeks back and they start to clap.

They go left right, left right, then I use my pussy muscles to make sure it's nice and tight.

I also like to lay on my side, as I enjoy the best ride.

Even though that's only a few,

I still know what I'd rather do.

I would rather be between there thighs, using my tongue to make their dick raise.

While I'm looking up into their eyes.

It makes me realize my mission here is complete,

I'd rather suck then fuck and no I'm not a slut, even though when I'm with my partner I like it in the butt.

I ENJOY

It's so big and thick,

I enjoy it deep in my throat,

I love to get it nice and soaked.

I get it so wet,

I be making all kinds of noises,

I slurp, I gargle, I swallow,

My jaw is very fit,

And no I don't spit.

My tongue has it's own tricks,

That will leave you speechless.

The looks on your face,

There so priceless.

I love when I bob my head faster and faster,

Making your moans get so intense,

You whisper under your breath "This shit makes no sense."

I love how you grab my hair,

Then you give me that stare.

Then you bust your nut,

I swallow it,

Now it's all in my gut.

YUMMY

You laid across the bed looking so yummy,

I laid my head down on your tummy.

I started licking on the tip of your dick,

Until, it got real nice and thick.

I laid in between your thighs sucking your dick,

Getting deeper and deeper, swallowing him whole,

At, this point I wanted to sit on your pole.

Riding him up and down, and around and around,

While listening to your moaning sound.

Then, you told me to get on all fours,

That it was your turn to make me sweat out of my pores.

You fucked me in my ass,

While grabbing my hair and holding my waist in the right place.

You continued the pounding until we busted our nut,

Damn, I love it when you fuck me in the butt.

MY MAN

My man likes it nasty,

He loves the fact that I'm a freak in the sheets,

But classy in the streets.

He knows I will always please,

I fulfill all his needs.

My man likes it nasty,

It doesn't matter if we are, fucking or I'm just sucking.

He knows all he has to do is ask,

Regardless of the sexual task.

I will do it without any hesitation or complaints.

My man likes it nasty,

We can go hours at a time,

Licking, kissing, spitting, rubbing, sucking, eating, fucking, slurping, gargling, swallowing.

I'm down for it all, my man loves to fuck me raw.

My man likes it nasty,

We will do it anywhere,

We don't care.

My man is my lover and my bestfriend and as long as we keep each other satisfied, we will have each other until the end of time.

My man likes it nasty,

He loves the fact that I'm a freak in the sheets,

But, classy in the streets.

He knows I will always please,

I fulfill all his needs.

I'M A GOAT

I'm a goat

When it comes to my throat

I'm sucking you're dick

While you're licking my clit

So passionate

I love to swallow him whole

He is a foot long pole

No gaggin'

No nuts saggin'

No beggin'

I'm a goat

When it comes to my throat

Swirl my tongue

Around and around

From the tip of your dick

I continue to lick

So passionate

I start to nibble

You start to giggle

I'm a goat

When it comes to my throat

I'm not done making love to your dick

It's so nice and thick

Hard as a brick

So passionate

I know your ready to cum

Yes, I love the taste as it slides down my throat

This isn't a joke

I'm a goat

When it comes to my throat

I want all of it

Not just some

No I don't spit

I see you moving your hips

So passionate

Then, you busted your nut

In my gut

Yessssss daddy it was so tasty

I just swallowed all your babies

I'm a goat

When it comes to my throat

SPIT ON IT

Spit on it, Lick on it, Suck on it, Get it driping wet

Spit rolling down my chin

The way I go in, you would think it's a sin

I love your dick

It's so nice and thick

Hard as a brick

12 inches in my throat

It's completely soaked

You're eyes rolling in the back of your head

While you're laying in your bed

I got you moaning my name

That shit is so insane

Spit on it, Lick on it, Suck on it, Get it driping wet

Spit rolling down my chin

The way I go in, you would think it's a sin

As I wrapped my fist around the bottom part of your dick

I squeezed it

As I bobbed my head faster and faster

Between each stroke

Don't worry baby I don't choke

My head game is far from a joke

I got you're legs shaking

I got you're toes curlin'

I can see the goosebumps all over you're body

Spit on it, Lick on it, Suck on it, Get it driping wet.

Spit rolling down my chin

The way I go in, you would think it's a sin

Twirling my tongue around and around

From the tip of your dick

I continue to Lick

All the way down

Until I can feel you're balls laying on my chin

Within seconds you busted your nut

All in my gut

Spit on it, Lick on it, Suck on it

Get it driping wet

Spit rolling down my chin

The way I go in, you would think it's a sin

SUCK

I love to suck your dick

It is so nice and thick

I enjoy licking the tip

I enjoy it so much

You know you never have to ask

I'm always down for that sexual task

I suck it, lick it, kiss it, fuck it, spit on it

I drown it with my juices

I swallow him whole

I get it so deep all the way down to my soul

Once he is hard and thick

I know he is at least 11 inches

And, it feels like a solid brick

I wrap my fingers around him

At the bottom so I can work him down my throat

And, oh he gets nice and soaked

I bob my head faster and faster

Your moan getting so intense

You moan you're about to nut all in my gut

It's the best taste ever

Sucking him is such amazing pleasure

FREAKY GIRL

You want to see a freaky girl

You want to see my pussy cream

Well my man is the only one to make me scream

He loves to play with my pussy

He gets me all wet and gushy

He knows how to please

He really enjoys it when I'm laying between his knees

Sucking his big thick dick

Yes it is nice and thick

I enjoy licking and kissing it

I also enjoy sucking on his balls licking them from the bottom all the way to the top

I could do this all day

Never stop

You want to see a freaky girl

You want to see my pussy cream

Well my man is the only one to make me scream

He bangs this pussy out

43

From the front and the back

That's a fact

He gets me moaning

Moaning his name

Our sex life is never a bore

Us together add up to a 100% score

You want to see a freaky girl

You want to see my pussy cream

Well my man is the only one to make me scream

I NEVER CHOKE

I want to lick you have head to toe

I'm never gonna let you go

Gently lick the creases of your inner thigh

Yeah I enjoy being with a freaky guy

Start sucking both of your balls at the same time

You will always be mine

I squeeze the dick at the bottom

Deep throating your dick

Swallowing it whole

Without gagging one bit

I Never choke

I keep it super soaked

Bobbing my head faster and faster

I look up at your eyes

There rolling in the back of your head

But that's no surprise

You tell me your about to cum all down my throat

I said, "OK boo, do what you do."

You squinted all down my throat

It tasted so yummy

I said boo, are you ready for round 2

Because I want some more of you.

REMINISCING

Sitting here reminiscing about the first night we met

We started kissing

That's the shit that I be missing

Weeks turned into days

Days turned into hours

That we couldn't go without seeing each other

You always knew how to cheer me up

You treated me differently

You knew I wasn't a slut

I always kept it real

Told you how I feel

As time went on

You realized I liked your dick in all 3 holes

Your dick feels like a solid pole

I enjoy it balls deep

I wish it could fit all the way down to my feet

But it's cool

I'm not a fool

No

I don't have to be schooled

I don't follow any rules

With 12 inches long

You got me moaning

Like I'm writing a love song

You whispered in my ears

You got me grinding my gears

In slow motion

You're pussy is squirting magic potion

It's super soaked

You tried so hard not to cum

But, with pussy like this

You couldn't help but squirt all in it

Sure enough you were finished

Sitting here reminiscing about the first night we met

We started kissing

That's the shit I be missing

DRIPPITY DROP

Drippity Drop Don't Stop

I got that dick on lock

Got him deep in my Throat

He is super soaked

You love it because I never choke

Drippity Drop Don't Stop

I got that dick on lock

At 1st it took you by surprise

And was in complete shock

That even with 12 itches long

And hard as a rock

My head continue to bop

Getting faster and faster

Gripping by tongue around him

No gagging at all

Drippity Drop Don't Stop

I got that dick on lock

Make it rain

While giving you brain

While your finger popping my pussy

Getting it all wet and gushy

Then you ask if you could slide

Your big ass dick in my tushy

I said, " Yes please " so I got on all 4's

Ass up face down

I love the fact you make me nut

While fucking my ass

I will forever be your beauty queen

My love for you is as exactly how it seems

You are my drug

And, you got me feeling like a fen

Drippity Drop Don't Stop

I got that dick on lock

Drippity Drippity Drip Drip Drop Don't Stop

I got that dick on lock

LET'S DO IT

Let's do it, let's do it,

Put your back into it.

Move your hips left to right,

Squeeze your pussy muscles nice & tight

It's going to be one amazing night

Ass up face down

Dick in the ass, make it last

Bust your nut, in my butt.

Clean it off,

Then, smack it, wiggle it, jiggle it

Flip me over, slide it in

You thought we were done,

Naw, we just begun.

Spread my legs apart,

Right from the start.

Lick me, kiss me, do me right

All through the night.

Don't nibble, just bite

You know I'm a freak in the bed

You know I enjoy giving head,

Sixty-nine,

We can do that all the time.

I go hours without complaints,

The look in his eyes,

Make me realize,

He enjoys this more each and everytime.

And, it's even better because we are together.

Making love all through the night,

Regardless of the weather

We will be one always and forever.

WHISPERS

You whispered in my ear that you wanted to pour chocolate syrup in my ass crack, and lick it from front to back

You, wanted me to hold ice cubes on your balls, as I sucked your dick,

The ice cubes make you cum so much, you love me more with very touch.

As, I whispered back to you, well I want to sit behind you with my legs wrapped around your waist, while I scoop my arms under your armpits and lean you in so tight,

I know you won't put up a fight.

I want to grind my pussy lips, all over your hips.

You flipped over, and poured candle wax all down my lower back.

While, I sucked on your nut sack.

Babe, we need to get on board, and start the complete body tour,

Get on all fours so we can fuck on the floor, all day and all night, while we stare into the candle light.

Damn, that's one amazing sight.

I WANT

I want to get up on your dick and sit.

I want to go in circles,

like a merry go round, I want to bounce up and down while you're sipping on your coke and crown.

Then, I want to shake my ass cheeks left right, left right,

while my pussy lips grip your dick nice and tight.

I'm all in for the long ride.

Once were done it will be a slip and slide.

Once,

I get up off your dick, our cum compound is very thick.

Then, it's time for me to go down to start licking, before it starts sticking.

Then, I started to stroke him, and he started to poke me.

I knew in that moment I wanted your dick to be deep in my throat so I can gargle your cum,

without gagging one bit.

Thank God he gave me the ability to be able to breathe through my nose and deep throat at the same time.

I love the taste of your cum while entwined with mine.

Yes, boo I'm ready for round two.

How about you?

DRIP

DRIP DRIP Drip Drip Drip

Make it wet,

Eat it up,

Don't stop until I bust a nut,

DRIP DRIP Drip Drip Drip

Now slide it in,

Fuck me good,

Grind that pussy like your hood,

DRIP DRIP Drip Drip Drip

Make it wet,

Slip & Slide,

Keep fucking me until I'm ready to ride,

DRIP DRIP Drip Drip Drip

Make it gushy,

All in my pussy,

Make it rain,

Make me feel like I'm insane

DRIP DRIP Drip Drip Drip

Now that I have cum,

I'm ready to give you some,

I get down on my knees,

I'm ready to please,

DRIP DRIP Drip Drip Drip

Your dick is as hard as a pole,

I'm ready to swallow him whole,

Deep throat,

No gagging,

DRIP DRIP Drip Drip Drip

Have you moaning my name,

Now that shit is insane,

Now bust your nut,

In my gut,

DRIP DRIP Drip Drip Drip

DRIP DRIP Drip Drip Drip

DRIP DRIP Drip Drip Drip

ABOUT THE AUTHOR

My name is Beans Lee. I am 41 years old. I'm from Annapolis MD. I have one daughter and one grandson. I am a Mother, Nana, Auntie, Sister, Friend, Author, and a Poet. I suffer from multiple Chronic Pain Disorders, as well as Mental health disorders, such as Anxiety and Depression, PTSD and etc. I started writing poetry when I was just 12 years old. My books will have many volumes because I want to share all types of my poetry with my friends, family and my fans. I started sharing and performing my poetry over 6 years ago. I'm starting with the vivid sexual poems, because that is how I started performing live. And, have gained my fan base. I hope each person that reads my books, find it helpful in some kind of situation that they can relate to. Thank you for purchasing my first poetry book! Love Always, Beans Lee!

Made in the USA
Middletown, DE
23 October 2023

41194686R00036